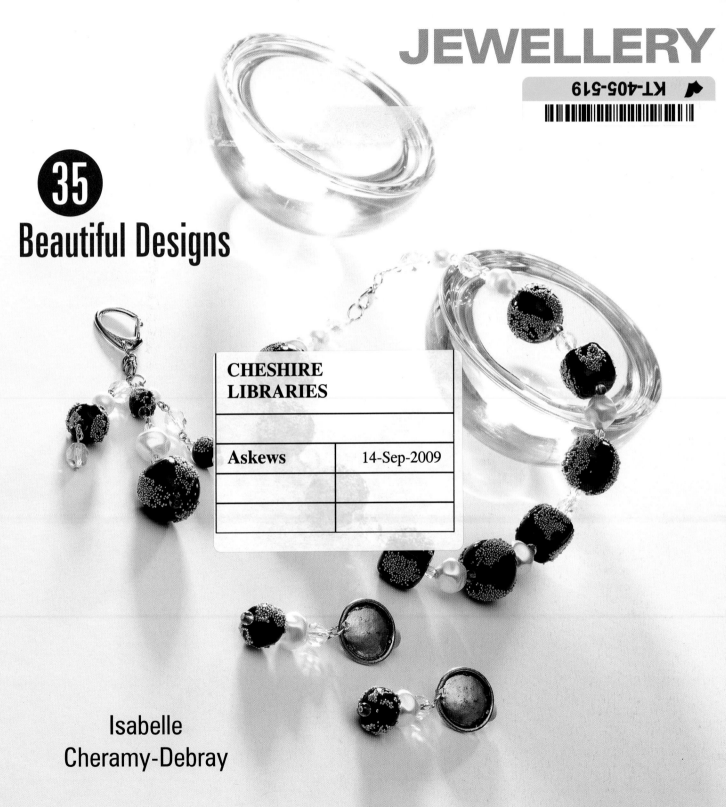

Polymer Clay
Beaded
JEWELLERY

35
Beautiful Designs

Isabelle
Cheramy-Debray

Search Press

Contents

Foreword 2
Polymer clay 3
Materials and Supplies
for working with jewellery 4
Glossary 5
Materials and Supplies
for working with polymer clay 6

The jewellery

8
Watercolour

12
Savannah

16
Marina

20
Primrose

24
Venice

28
Moonlight

31
Rosebud

34
Coral

37
Trump heart

40
Harlequin

44
Tenderness

Photographs of the jewellery by Rémi Dazin, *PepperMilk*

To my mother, for her unconditional support
To Patrice, my husband, for his wise words and patience
To Pauline and Gauthier, my children, my two rays of sunshine

Foreword

My great passion for making unusual jewellery has now been extended to include polymer clay.

The first word that comes to mind when I think of this clay is 'magic'. There are so many shapes, textures, colours and designs to explore and share with you.

The techniques presented in this book can be used to make any number of creations, and I hope that you will very quickly be able to create your own designs.

I am lucky enough to regularly meet people who have been inspired by my work, and it gives me great pleasure to see some of their colourful creations. The purpose of this book is not only to introduce you to making beads in polymer clay, but also to show you how to make the jewellery itself.

A beautiful piece of jewellery is not simply a lovely creation to admire, it is also timeless, durable and easy to wear. The finishes are therefore described in detail for every piece.

I hope that you will find as much pleasure as I do in the marvellous world of making jewellery from polymer clay.

Isabelle

The author would like to thank the following:
Fiskars and Décopatch
for the Fimo clay;
DTM and Eberhard Faber
for the Sculpey and the magenta stamps;
Hubinont Hobby
for Diam's products;
Oz International
for the Tulip products;
Colart for the Ranger products
(Perfect Pearls and alcoholic ink);
Acicam for Makin's Clay products;
Kars for Désiré threads;
and DMC.

The author would also like to thank all the team at Éditions Didier Carpentier, particularly Marie Delauney for her invaluable help in writing each new book.

Polymer clay

Invented in the 1940s, polymer clay is essentially made
from minuscule particles of polyvinyl chloride (PVC)
suspended in a petroleum distillate compound.
Originally used to make dolls and miniatures, it is used
today in various creative processes, such as making decorative objects or jewellery.

There are many different brands of polymer clay available, such as Fimo, Sculpey, Cernit, Premo, etc.
We have selected two brands for making beads: Sculpey III and Fimo Soft.
These two types of clay are fairly pliable to work with and come in a very wide range of colours
and finishes (matt, metallic, iridescent, transparent, etc.)
However, Fimo Classic is recommended for millefiori work.
This clay is firmer and is less likely to lose its shape when you are making motifs.
As real modelling clay, it can be sculpted, rolled, cut out or painted as you wish. Available in a 60g (2oz) block,
you will also find some colours in larger sizes. All the amounts in this book are based on standard blocks.

Caution
This modelling clay should be used by children only if they are over the age of eight
years old and are under the supervision of an adult. It should not be placed in the mouth.
The work surface must be cleaned after use as well as all the utensils,
which should be used solely for that purpose.

Preparation of the clay

Before doing anything else, start by kneading the polymer clay
to make it pliable. Roll it out on your work surface, fold it, roll it
again and continue until the clay is really flexible, smooth and
uniform. The heat of your hand will make the clay pliable,
making it easier to work with. You can also use a pasta
machine (see page 6).

Should the clay be old or difficult to work, you can use
softeners. Available in blocks, you just mix them with the
traditional clay, taking care not to exceed a certain percentage
recommended by the manufacturer. In general, the proportion
is a maximum of one-third softener to two-thirds clay. The
product does not alter the colour.

Rolling out the clay

This can be done on a work surface of your choice, either
a simple tile or a plate of glass. There are two ways of
rolling out the clay: using a roller/by hand, and using a
pasta machine.

- Using a roller/by hand
This is the traditional method. A simple glass bottle is perfect,
but you can also use a plastic tube. Avoid using a wooden
rolling pin as the fibres will not only spoil the clay, but will
also make it stick to the rolling pin. Furthermore, any
object used to work the polymer clay must not be used for
culinary purposes.

- Using a pasta machine
This has the advantage of quickly producing a smooth and
regular sheet. Always start by spacing the wheels of the
machine as far apart as possible, then gradually reducing
the gap to obtain the desired thickness. Pasta machines are
not all the same and the graduations will differ from model
to model.

Tips
As polymer clay is very fine, always ensure that you wash your
hands thoroughly after each use, as well as the work surface
(with a damp cloth or baby wipe), so that you do not spoil any
new clay.

Decorating the clay

Many different products can be used to decorate polymer clay.
You will usually find them in the scrapbooking section of craft shops.

- Powders:
These are made from fine metallic or iridescent particles of mica, and
are usually gold, silver or copper in colour.
Perfect Pearls is an example of one brand on the market that offers a
wide range of colours.
These powders are very useful for inclusions or to give a surface a
metallic effect (see Moonlight on page 28).

- Dimensional painting:
Traditionally used to customise clothes, its use has now been extended
to more varied surfaces, including polymer clay.
This quick-drying paint is easy to apply and is available in a wide
range of colours and finishes (gloss, iridescent, matt and sparkling).
It is ideal for raised decoration (see Tenderness on page 44).
It can only be applied after baking, and can be varnished.

- Textured sheets:
These are available mainly from Fiskars or Makin's Clay and are used
to reproduce various textures on sheets of paper by exerting pressure.
We have used several types when making the Moonlight design
(see page 28).

- Decorative stamps:
With their wide range of motifs, decorative stamps are used for
printing original shapes in the clay using inks (see Savannah on
page 12), or for creating moulds for false enamel (see Primrose
on page 20).

- Cutters:
These are used for cutting out various shapes in different sizes easily
and accurately to make original pieces (see Rosebud on page 31).

Sanding

Sanding enables you to remove any irregularities and fingerprints.
This is a very important part of the finishing process, ensuring the
beauty of the beads. Industrial grade sandpaper is ideal: numbers
400 and 600 to start with, and numbers 800 and 1200 for a
lacquered effect.
Allow the sandpaper to soak in water before use. Prepare a small
basin of warm water and add some washing-up liquid. Sand your
object and dip it regularly in the warm water to see how the sanding
is progressing. Finish by rinsing in clean water.

Polymer clay

Baking

A simple, household oven will bake all your creations at a temperature of 110° or 130°C, according to the manufacturer's specific instructions. It is very important not to exceed the temperature indicated so as to avoid the release of toxic fumes. A thermometer can help you to keep to the exact temperature. A fan oven will improve the baking.

Should overheating occur and cause the inhalation of toxic fumes, ventilate the room, open the oven door and leave the room. Should any irritation occur (skin, throat, eyes, etc.), consult a doctor immediately.

Usually, a baking time of 20–30 minutes will be sufficient, but you can bake a piece several times if you wish – in order to add elements, for example. Make sure that you do not exceed 20–30 minutes for the new baking session. Transparent colours generally take less time to bake.

As clay will stick to metal, it is advisable to use a baking tray covered with greaseproof paper.

When the correct baking time has been reached, take the tray out of the oven and leave it to cool. Handle it with care as hot clay straight from the oven can easily lose its shape.

A container filled with iced water can be used to cool the clay instantly, to accentuate its transparency (if using translucent clay) or to create a cracked effect.

After this stage, the beads can be kept indefinitely. They are washable and impermeable to water.

Never bake clay in a microwave oven.

Varnishing

Each piece can be left in its natural state after baking as the clay will be hard enough. The application of varnish is purely for aesthetic reasons rather than for protection. However, when making beads, motifs, buttons, rings or brooches, we do recommend varnishing as it accentuates the effects of the materials, contours and colours (see right).

Without varnish　　*With varnish*

Never use nail varnish on polymer clay as it contains solvents that attack the clay and make it sticky. Most suppliers have a special polymer varnish (which can be removed with water or white spirit). For jewellery, we advise that cleaning is done with white spirit, which is more resistant to friction.

To make the varnishing easier, thread your beads on to cocktail sticks and stick them into a block of foam or polystyrene while drying. Use pegs for hair clips or rings.

There are two ways of varnishing your beads: using a paintbrush or by placing them in a special bath.

If you use a paintbrush, make sure that you varnish all the surfaces of the bead and rinse the brush with white spirit immediately after use. (The special polymer varnish dries very quickly and will spoil the bristles of the brush if not cleaned off at once.)

With a special bath, you just need to immerse your beads in the bottle of varnish having carefully threaded them on to wooden sticks beforehand. The benefit of this method is that it leaves a fairly thick layer of varnish and avoids the need for a second layer. However, as the risk of unsightly runs is greater, ensure that you turn your beads regularly while they are drying.

Storage

Polymer clay can be kept for a long time provided you follow certain rules. When exposed to air, the clay hardens and crumbles, and so it must therefore be kept in an airtight box or glass jar, which will also protect it from dust. Wrap each block of clay in greaseproof paper or cling film (see right) so that the colours do not mix. Do not place clay that has not hardened on to varnished or plastic surfaces.

1 - Ribbons and fancy wool
In this book, we mainly use chiffon or satin ribbons and furry knitting yarn.

2 - Linked chains of varying thicknesses
These serve to extend a piece of jewellery or become the finding to be decorated.

3 - Locking or crimping beads
Small metal beads that you crimp on the thread.

4 - Metal chokers
Circular metal with screw fastening in the shape of a ball.

5 - Flat head pins
These are simple pins (or joining pins) or pins with a flat head with which you can make a loop using round-nosed pliers.

6 - Cable wire
Made of several stainless steel wires twisted and covered with a nylon sheath. They are available in various shades. We mainly use silver wire that is 0.46mm in diameter.

7 - Copper wire sheathed in cotton
This new wire, recently developed by DMC, has the advantage of both holding its shape and coming in a variety of colours, including those with a satin finish.

8 - Ring findings with a flat surface
These are rings with a flat base ready to be decorated by sticking on a simple addition made from polymer clay.

9 - Scalloped tulip beads
These are used to hide knots, drawing together several threads.

10 - Fancy glass beads
Available in a very wide range of shapes and colours, these complement some polymer clay designs perfectly, e.g. with a pearly or transparent effect.

11 - Rocaille beads
These are the most commonly used beads and come in a very wide variety of colours and finishes (iridescent, metallic, opaque, etc.). They are inexpensive and easy to find.

12 - Clip-on earrings
These are the bases for earrings that clip on the ears. They come in many shapes and colours.

13 - Rings
These are made from metal and are open so that something can be inserted. They come in various diameters.

14 - Clasps
These are indispensable accessories. We recommend that you use 13mm (½in) long lobster clasps, as they can be used for both necklaces and bracelets. Fancy double clasps are also useful.

15 - Knot covers
These are shells used to hide finishing knots.

16 - Cutting pliers

17 - Flat-nosed pliers
An indispensable tool for flattening metal pieces or for opening rings.

18 - Conical or round pliers
These are used to make the loops on flat head pins.

19 - Leather crimps for braid
These are flat knot covers that can be adapted for various uses (braid, ribbons, cord, etc.).

20 - Sleepers
These are the bases of earrings for pierced ears.

21 - Chain tassels
With their little loops, these can easily be attached to jewellery.

22 - Hair clip findings
These are sprung clips, 5–8cm (2–3¼in) in length, ready for decorating.

23 - Keyrings

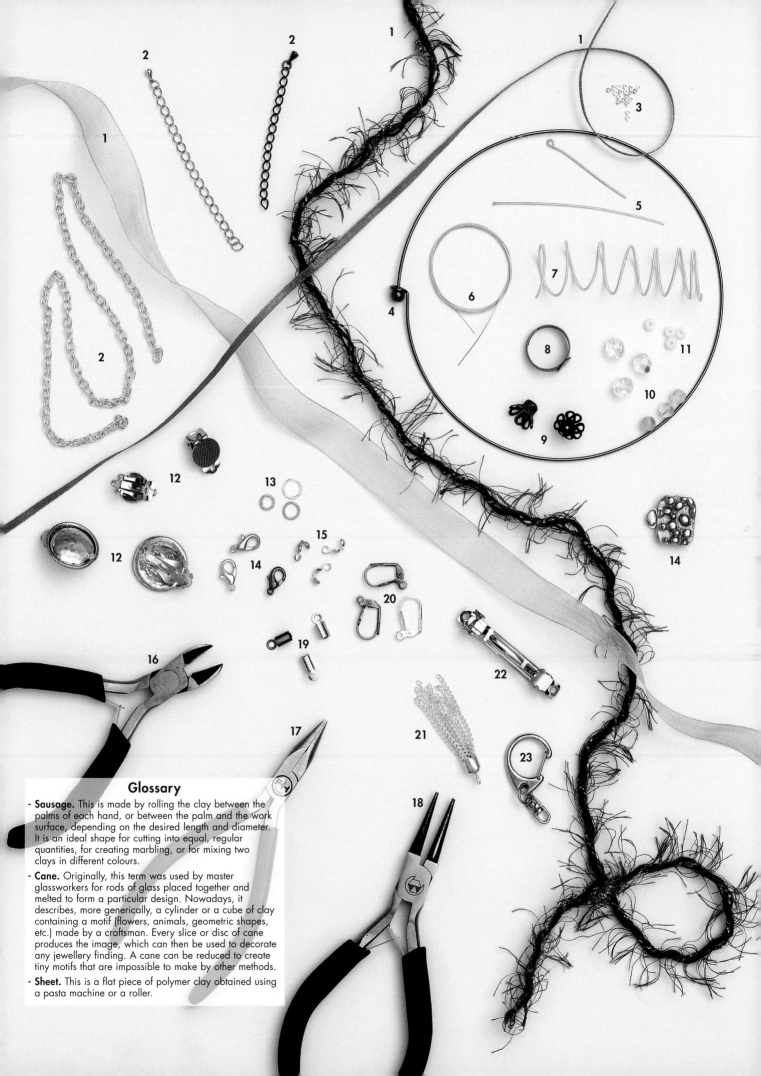

Glossary

- **Sausage.** This is made by rolling the clay between the palms of each hand, or between the palm and the work surface, depending on the desired length and diameter. It is an ideal shape for cutting into equal, regular quantities, for creating marbling, or for mixing two clays in different colours.

- **Cane.** Originally, this term was used by master glassworkers for rods of glass placed together and melted to form a particular design. Nowadays, it describes, more generically, a cylinder or a cube of clay containing a motif (flowers, animals, geometric shapes, etc.) made by a craftsman. Every slice or disc of cane produces the image, which can then be used to decorate any jewellery finding. A cane can be reduced to create tiny motifs that are impossible to make by other methods.

- **Sheet.** This is a flat piece of polymer clay obtained using a pasta machine or a roller.

Materials and Supplies
for working with polymer clay

1 - **Sandpaper (dry or special industrial paper numbers 400–1200).** *These enable you to obtain a nice finish, in some instances even approaching that of a lacquer (with a gloss varnish).*

2 - **Microbeads.** *These are tiny glass balls that we stick to the polymer clay.*

3 - **Coloured sand.** *Traditionally used for collage with pictures, coloured sand enables you to colour and give a distinctive texture to polymer clay. A wide range of colours is available.*

4 - **Polymer clay blocks.** *Available in various shades and finishes (matt, iridescent, transparent, fluorescent and metallic), the most commonly available block weighs 60g (2oz) and is pre-cut into eight pieces. Larger sized blocks are available, but in a more limited range of colours.*

5 - **Ruler.**

6 - **Craft knife.** *Standard or precision, this is an indispensable cutting tool.*

7 - **Clay gun.** *This is a metal syringe that is filled with clay to make fine sausages in various shapes depending on the nozzle selected (round, square, etc.).*

8 - **Sticks, needles or various pliers (e.g. cocktail stick, wooden skewer, peg, etc.).** *These are used for piercing or for holding beads and jewellery.*

9 - **Dimensional paint.** *Usually used for decorating clothes, this is ideal for decorating baked beads with a raised design. It can be iridescent, sparkling, matt, etc., and comes in a range of colours.*

10 - **Alcohol ink.** *This is ideal for mixing with liquid polymer clay as it produces a certain transparency, which is good for making false enamels. One of the most well known brands is Ranger.*

11 - **Cutters.** *These are made from plastic or metal in all sorts of shapes. You'll find them in the modelling section, as well as with the kitchen utensils. The Makin's Clay brand from the USA has a very wide choice.*

12 - **Ink pads.** *These are available in various colours, rapid or slow drying, for use with ink stamps.*

13 - **Ink stamps.** *An easy way to alter the texture of the clay, these are also used for printing motifs.*

14 - **Cling film.** *Place it over the polymer clay at the start. It makes it easier to cut out the clay using cutters (it keeps the edges sharp). It is indispensable for storing canes (see Glossary on page 5).*

15 - **Greaseproof paper.** *This is used to prevent the polymer clay from sticking to the baking tray.*

16 - **Brushes.**

17 - **Metal findings.** *Specially designed for polymer clay, these enable the imitation of enamels. They are available in square or round shapes under the Eberhard Faber brand.*

18 - **Pastry wheel.** *Usually used for cutting shapes in pastry, these are also useful for cutting shapes out of polymer clay.*

19 - **Superglue.** *This is ideal for sticking a polymer clay piece to a metal base, such as a hair slide or ring.*

20 - **Metallic leaves.** *These are ideal for making inclusions or covering beads. They are most commonly available in gold, silver or multicoloured flakes.*

21 - **Snail plate.** *The depressions in the tin can be used to give a convex form to polymer clay beads.*

22 - **Powder.** *Available in gold, silver or bronze, these give a metallic look to the finished item. New and more unusual colours can be found under the Perfect Pearls brand.*

23 - **Special ink stamp cleaner.** *A lotion that completely removes all encrusted ink from the surface of the stamp.*

24 - **Varnish.** *Finishing product that brings out the colours or the raised design. Available in gloss or satin finishes and water- or solvent-based. We mainly use the gloss, solvent-based varnish.*

25 - **Liquid polymer clay.** *A transparent liquid used for sticking, filling or glazing items in traditional polymer clay.*

26 - **Patterned sheets of paper.** *They are applied to the polymer clay for decoration.*

27 - **Paper adhesive.** *Traditional adhesive used for working with paper.*

28 - **Textured sheets.** *Simple plastic sheets in various designs, these are often used for scrapbooking to emboss paper.*

29 - **Pasta machine.** *You will find this in the cookware department. It is used to roll out the clay quickly in regular sheets of varying thicknesses.*

30 - **Polystyrene block (or egg box).** *This is used to hold the cocktail sticks in place while you thread the beads on to them for varnishing or painting.*

31 - **Pliable, heart-shaped mould.**

Not shown in the photograph

Tile or glass sheet. *Both are very useful as work surfaces. With their smooth surfaces, both are easy to clean and will not leave a pattern on the clay.*

Oven thermometer. *This gives the exact temperature, being independent of the oven itself.*

Latex gloves. *These prevent fingerprints from being left on the clay when it is being worked.*

Watercolour

Colours and quantities of clay used

pale pistachio green (10g/½oz) – mint blue (small lump) – cherry red (7.5g/¼oz) – white (45g/1½oz)
offcuts of clay in various colours (approximately 35g/1¼oz)*

Other materials

clay gun

Making the BEADS

Start by kneading the various clays on the glass sheet to make them pliable and then make a ball in each colour (keep any offcuts to one side).

Then cut:
- the white clay ball into three pieces (**V**, **W**, **X**); then cut piece **X** into two pieces (one-third to be **X1** and two-thirds to form **X2**)
- the red clay ball into two pieces (**Y**, **Z**); then cut piece **Z** into two (**Z1** and **Z2**).

Mix together the following in order to make balls in different colours:
- **pink:** the piece of white clay **X2** with the piece of red clay **Z2**
- **raspberry:** the piece of white clay **X1** with the piece of red clay **Z1**
- **light blue:** the piece of white clay **W** with the mint blue ball **U**.

Once these balls have been formed, make sausages of approximately 1cm (½in) in diameter. Do the same with the piece of white clay **V**, the red clay **Y**, and the pistachio green ball **T**. You should have six sausages.

Cut each sausage into sections 0.5–1cm (¼–½in) long. Prepare the clay gun by selecting the multiholed tip in the largest size.

Assemble a sausage approximately 6cm (2¼in) long with the discs thus formed of every different colour of clay, ensuring that you distribute the different colours well.

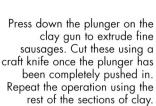

Roll the sausage gently on the work surface so that the sections stick well to one another. Slide the sausage into the clay gun.

Press down the plunger on the clay gun to extrude fine sausages. Cut these using a craft knife once the plunger has been completely pushed in. Repeat the operation using the rest of the sections of clay.

When working with polymer clay, there are always a lot of offcuts. Keep them to one side, as they will be useful for making particular items, such as those described here.

Watercolour

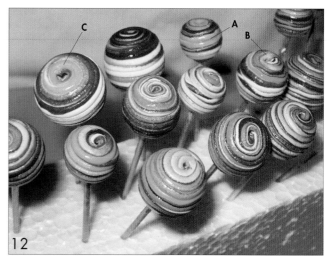

Make a ball by mixing the offcuts of clay (in any colour) and then make a sausage 1cm (½in) in diameter.

Cut five sections 8mm (¼in) long for beads **A**, fourteen sections 1.5cm (¾in) long for beads **B** and three sections 3cm (1¼in) long for beads **C**.

Make a ball with each section to make the centre of each bead.

Start to make the covering by applying the end of a sausage of clay to the top of each of the various balls.

Press down gently to make it stick, then turn it around evenly in order to cover the whole ball (see above).

Cut off the excess sausage using the craft knife.

Press gently on to each ball to make sure that everything is firmly in place.

Pierce each ball with a needle. Place each one on a sheet of greaseproof paper and bake in the oven for the time recommended by the manufacturer.

Once they have completely cooled, place the balls on cocktail sticks, so that you can work with them more easily.

Apply two layers of varnish to each ball.

Press the sticks into a polystyrene block and leave to dry.

KEYRING

Length: 9.5cm (3¾in)

MATERIALS

1 bead **A** – 2 beads **B** – 1 ring, diameter 7mm (silver), **Y'** – 2 transparent beads, diameter 6mm (blue), **b**
3 transparent beads, diameter 6mm (green), **v** – 1 joining pin (silver), **T** – 2 flat head pins (silver), **T'**
1 keyring shank (silver) – 20cm (7¾in) of 3mm (⅛in) wide satin ribbon (fuchsia)

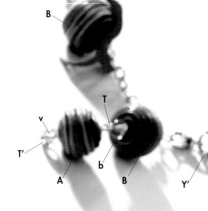

Prepare two charms on the flat head pins **T'**:
– on to charm 1, thread one **v** bead and the **A** bead
– on to charm 2, thread one **b** bead, one **B** bead and one **v** bead.

Leave 7mm (¼in) of the pin free, cut off the excess, and make a loop using conical pliers. Thread on to the joining pin **T** the following beads: one **b**; one **B**; and one **v**.

Make a loop at each end, in the same way as for the pins **T'**. Attach charm 2 to one of the ends of the chain.

Then assemble charm 1 with pin **T**. Open ring **Y'** and slip on the two charms. Then attach **Y'** to the keyring shank. Tie the satin ribbon on to charm 2.

EARRINGS

Length of earring: 6cm (2¼in)

2 beads **B**
2 flat head pins **T'**
2 transparent beads, diameter 6mm (blue), **b**
2 transparent beads, diameter 6mm (green), **v**
2 pieces of chain 1.5cm (¾in) long (silver)
1 pair of sleepers (silver)

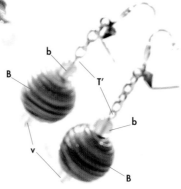

Thread the following beads on to one of the **T'** pins: one **v**; one **B**; and one **b**.

Cut off the excess pin, leaving just the 7mm (¼in) necessary to make a loop using the conical pliers.

Take a piece of chain and slide one of its ends on to the loop.

Open the little ring located at the base of one of the sleepers and slide the other end of the chain on to this ring.

Make the other earring in the same way.

Watercolour

NECKLACE
Length: 55cm (21¾in)

MATERIALS

2 beads **A** – 4 round beads **B** – 3 round beads **C** – 9 joining pins (silver)
9 transparent beads, diameter 6mm (blue), **b** – 1 lobster claw clasp (silver)
9 transparent beads, diameter 6mm (green), **v**
2 rings, diameter 5mm (silver), **Y**
30cm (12in) of 3mm (⅛in) wide satin ribbon (fuchsia)

Start by preparing the various joining pins:
Thread on to two of the **A'** pins the following beads:
one **b**; one **A**; and one **v**
on to four of the **B'** pins: one **b**; one **B**; and one **v**
on to three of the **C'** pins: one **b**; one **C**; and one **v**.

Cut the end off each pin to leave just the 7mm (¼in)
needed to make a loop. Make each loop using the
conical pliers.

Divide the chain into 10 × 2.5cm (1in) long pieces. Put the
various pieces together in the following order, inserting a piece
of chain between each pin: one **A'** pin; two **B'** pins; three **C'**
pins; two **B'** pins; and one **A'** pin.

Attach a **Y** ring to each end, and then attach the lobster claw
clasp between the two rings.

Cut the ribbon into four equal pieces. Attach the first piece to the
second pin from one end, the second piece to the fourth pin,
and continue thus, every other pin, to the end of the necklace.

BRACELET
Length: 23cm (9in)

2 beads **A** – 6 round beads **B** – 5 transparent beads, diameter 6mm (blue), **b**
5 transparent beads, diameter 6mm (green), **v** – 2.5cm (1in) of chain (silver)
2 rings, diameter 7mm (silver), **Y'** – 1 flat head pin (silver), **T'**
2 locking beads (silver), **p** – 1 lobster claw clasp (silver)
25cm (9¾in) cable wire, diameter 0.46mm (silver)

Thread a locking bead **p** and the lobster claw clasp on to one end of the
cable wire. Pass 2cm (¾in) of the end of the cable wire back through bead **p**
and crimp the bead with the flat-nosed pliers.

Then thread on the beads in the following order: one **b**; one **A**; *one **v**; one
B; one **b**; one **B***. Repeat twice from * to *; then one **v**; one **A**; and one **b**.
End with one **p** and one **Y'**.

Pass the wire back through the locking bead **p** and through the last two
threaded beads. Crimp the bead **p** with the flat-nosed pliers. Cut off the
excess wire. Attach one **Y'** ring to one end of the chain, and then fix the other
end to the **Y'** ring already attached.

Thread one **v** bead on to pin **T'**. Make a loop at the end and then attach it to
the free **Y'** ring at the end of the chain.

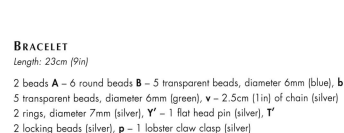

Savannah

Colours and quantities of clay used

iridescent white (30g/1oz) – copper brown (7.5g/¼oz) – liquid polymer clay

Other materials and equipment

3 flower-shaped cutters, diameters 2cm (¾in), 3cm (1¼in) and 4cm (1½in)– 1 stamp with foliage motif 4cm (1½in) long –
1 stamp with calligraphy motif 9 × 13cm (3½ × 5in)
2 ink pads (gold and sepia) – 1 special stamp cleaner (or special lotion) – 1 clay gun – 1 skewer – 1 adjustable ring finding (copper)

Making the MOTIFS

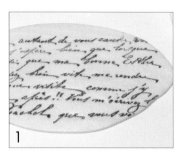

Prepare your iridescent white clay by kneading it and then rolling it out with a roller or using the pasta machine to make a rectangle 9 × 13cm (3½ × 5in). Cover the calligraphy motif stamp with sepia ink and then apply it to the sheet of clay. Press gently on each corner of the stamp so that the whole motif is properly transferred.

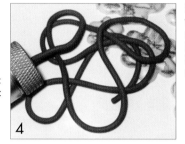

Knead the copper brown clay well. Prepare the clay gun by selecting the right tip to make 2mm (¹⁄₁₆in) diameter sausages. Slide the clay into the gun and make a long sausage.

Continue in the same way with the gold ink and corresponding stamp for the foliage motif, transferring it several times.

Leave to dry for a few minutes and carefully clean each stamp used with the special lotion.

Use the 4cm (1½in) diameter cutter on the decorated clay to make flower motif **A**, the 3cm (1¼in) diameter cutter to make four **B** motifs, and the 2cm (¾in) diameter cutter to make three **C** motifs.

Carefully remove the excess clay from around the flower motifs and place them in a cool place. This will enable you to work with them more easily without distorting their shape.

Apply pieces of copper brown sausage clay around each motif. Mark the angles with a skewer. Gently smooth out each contour.

Take a needle, then make a hole in two ends of motif **A** and in one of the **B** motifs. Then make a hole in just one end of five other motifs (two **B**s and three **C**s). Bake in the oven for the time recommended by the manufacturer.

Making the RING *Diameter: 3 cm (1¼in)*

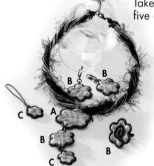

Take the **B** motif without a hole and decorate the top of it with an offcut of sausage clay.

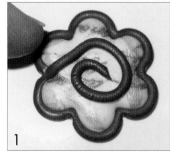

Turn the motif over and place the ring finding on to it, pressing down gently. Apply a little liquid polymer clay all around the base of the finding to strengthen the piece. Place the piece on a sheet of greaseproof paper and bake it in the oven for the time recommended by the manufacturer.

Savannah

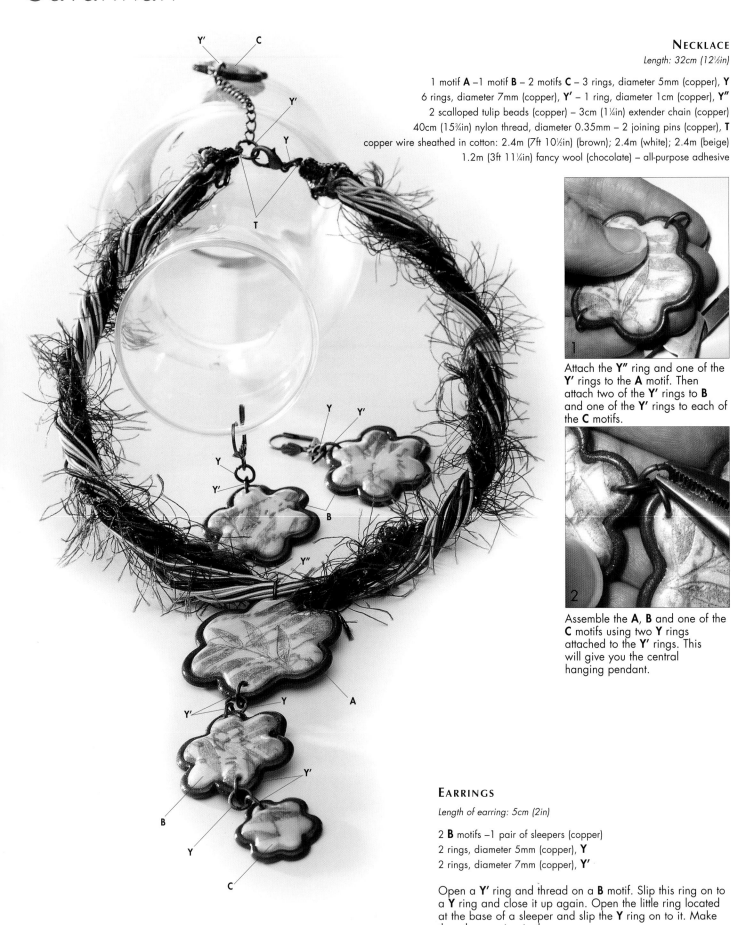

Length: 32cm (12½in)

1 motif **A** – 1 motif **B** – 2 motifs **C** – 3 rings, diameter 5mm (copper), **Y**
6 rings, diameter 7mm (copper), **Y'** – 1 ring, diameter 1cm (copper), **Y"**
2 scalloped tulip beads (copper) – 3cm (1¼in) extender chain (copper)
40cm (15¾in) nylon thread, diameter 0.35mm – 2 joining pins (copper), **T**
copper wire sheathed in cotton: 2.4m (7ft 10½in) (brown); 2.4m (white); 2.4m (beige)
1.2m (3ft 11¼in) fancy wool (chocolate) – all-purpose adhesive

Attach the **Y"** ring and one of the **Y'** rings to the **A** motif. Then attach two of the **Y'** rings to **B** and one of the **Y'** rings to each of the **C** motifs.

Assemble the **A**, **B** and one of the **C** motifs using two **Y** rings attached to the **Y'** rings. This will give you the central hanging pendant.

EARRINGS

Length of earring: 5cm (2in)

2 **B** motifs – 1 pair of sleepers (copper)
2 rings, diameter 5mm (copper), **Y**
2 rings, diameter 7mm (copper), **Y'**

Open a **Y'** ring and thread on a **B** motif. Slip this ring on to a **Y** ring and close it up again. Open the little ring located at the base of a sleeper and slip the **Y** ring on to it. Make the other earring in the same way.

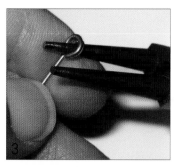

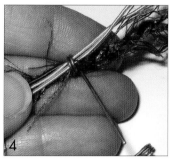

Prepare the fastenings by making a double loop 6mm (½in) in diameter at one end of each pin using the conical pliers.

Gather the ends of the three sheathed copper wires and the end of the fancy wool into the loop of a pin.

Bend them back over and twist the four strands together as close as possible to the loop of the pin. This process will temporarily hold the start of the work.

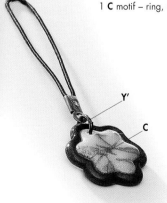

Thread the four strands, one by one, into the **Y"** ring of the hanging pendant, 20cm (7¾in) from the start of the work. Then, 20cm (7¾in) further on, thread the four strands in the same way into the loop of the second pin. After passing the strand of wool into the loop of the second pin, tie a knot as close as possible to the loop. Cut off the excess leaving just 2cm (¾in) remaining.

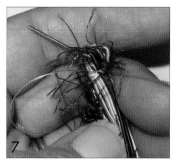

Firmly wrap a piece of nylon thread around the end of all of the threads, as close as possible to the loop of each pin. Make several knots and cut them, leaving 2cm (¾in) remaining.

Add a few drops of all-purpose adhesive to strengthen the knots. Leave to dry.

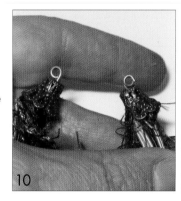

Thread the scalloped tulips on to each pin to hide the knots.

Make a double loop at the other end of each pin using the conical pliers. Attach a **Y** ring on a clasp to one of the ends, and a **Y'** ring attached to the chain to the other. Attach the second **C** motif to the other end of the chain using its **Y'** ring. Give the necklace its final shape by gently rolling the strands over one another from one end to the other.

FLOWER PENDANT
Length: 7.5cm (3in)

1 **C** motif – ring, diameter 7mm (copper), **Y'** – 10cm (4in) copper wire sheathed in cotton (brown) – 1 leather crimp for braid (copper)

Gather together the two ends of the sheathed wire. Twist them together two or three times, then slip them into the leather crimp. Pinch shut using the flat-nosed pliers.

Slip the **Y'** ring into the hole of the **C** motif, then into the little ring on the leather crimp.

Marina

Colours and quantities of clay used

transparent white (45g/1½oz)
metallic blue (22.5g/¾oz)
pastel aqua blue (7.5g/¼oz)
turquoise mint blue (7.5g/¼oz)
liquid polymer clay

Other materials and equipment

2 sheets of silver leaf
16 metal findings, diameter 2.5cm (1in) (silver)
16 joining pins (silver)
1 ring finding, diameter 2cm (¾in) (silver)

Making the Beads and the Ring

Knead the different clays to make them pliable, and then make a ball in each colour.

Flatten the balls of pastel aqua blue and turquoise mint blue to make sheets 13 × 5cm (5 × 2in) in area and 1mm (½₂in) thick. Repeat this process for the transparent white and metallic blue balls to make sheets 26 × 5cm (10¼ × 2in) and 1mm (½₂in) thick. Cut these last two sheets into two equal pieces.

Apply a sheet of silver leaf to the two rectangles of white clay. Smooth down well using your fingers to ensure that there are no air bubbles. Using the craft knife, cut off the excess silver leaf.

On top of the silver leaf/white rectangle, lay the pastel aqua blue sheet, one of the metallic blue sheets, the turquoise mint blue sheet, the second sheet of silver leaf/white clay, and the second sheet of metallic blue clay.

Cut the resultant block into two equal pieces. Lay one of these on top of the other, with the two metallic blue sides in the middle (see left). Line up the edges of this piece with your fingers to make a 5 × 7cm (2 × 2¾in) block.

Marina

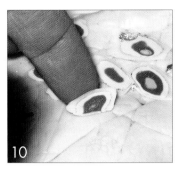

Turn the block over and apply the pieces of clay previously removed (see left). Then flatten the block to obtain a rectangle 16 × 9cm (6¼ × 3½in) and 3mm (⅛in) thick.

Take a ruler and gently press its side down into the block, proceeding across the block to mark out a rough grid. Then press the point of a ballpoint pen into each grid square (see left).

Place the 2.5cm (1in) diameter metal findings on to the block to make 16 **A** beads. Also include the silver ring finding (see left).

Press each side of the block with your fingers to fill up the holes you have just made. Then make a new grid and holes with the ballpoint pen on the other side of the block.

Press the 2.5cm (1in) diameter metal findings down into the clay using a roller.

Gently remove the excess clay around each finding, then place them in a cool place to prevent them from losing their shape when pierced. Wait a few minutes, then pierce them using the joining pins and the holes already there in each metal finding. Leave the pins in place for baking.

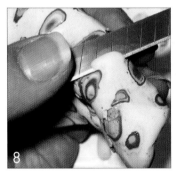

Gently flatten out the block with a roller until it is 1cm (½in) thick.

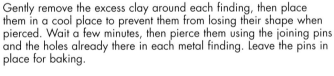

Mould the block of clay around your finger so that it takes on its shape. This will give you a tube, from which you can easily cut out different-sized pieces of clay using the craft knife (see left). Vary the depth of the cut from 2–5mm (¹⁄₁₆–¼in) over the whole surface of the block to expose the colours of the different clays. Keep all the pieces of clay thus removed.

Press the silver ring finding into the clay. Pull out the inlaid clay, place some drops of liquid polymer clay into the ring finding, then gently replace the piece of clay.

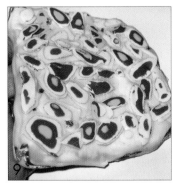

You will have formed irregular craters over the whole surface of the block.

Bake the beads and the ring in the oven for the time recommended by the manufacturer. Then plunge the beads and the ring into a container of iced water (see left) to accentuate the transparent effect. Leave to dry.

Apply a layer of varnish to the beads and the silver ring, being careful not to get any on the metal findings.

Marina

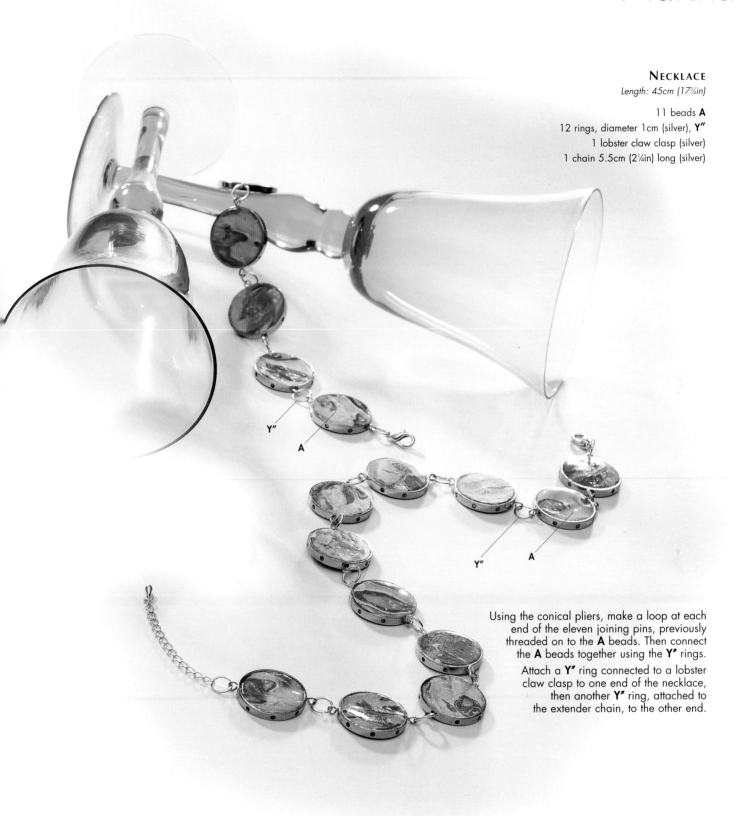

NECKLACE
Length: 45cm (17¾in)

11 beads **A**
12 rings, diameter 1cm (silver), **Y"**
1 lobster claw clasp (silver)
1 chain 5.5cm (2¼in) long (silver)

Y"

A

Y"

A

Using the conical pliers, make a loop at each end of the eleven joining pins, previously threaded on to the **A** beads. Then connect the **A** beads together using the **Y"** rings.

Attach a **Y"** ring connected to a lobster claw clasp to one end of the necklace, then another **Y"** ring, attached to the extender chain, to the other end.

BRACELET
Length: 22.5cm (8¾in)

5 beads **A** – 6 rings, diameter 1cm (silver), **Y"** – 1 lobster claw clasp (silver) – 1 chain 2.5cm (1in) long (silver)

Using the conical pliers, make a loop at each end of the five joining pins, previously threaded on to the **A** beads. Then attach the five **A** beads together, using the silver rings **Y"**.

Attach a **Y"** ring connected to the lobster claw clasp to one end of the bracelet, and another **Y"** ring, attached to the extender chain, to the other end.

Primrose

Information

This piece of jewellery is directly inspired by enamelling on metal, where the metal finding is hollowed out and then the hollows are filled with enamel.

Colours and quantities of clay used

offcuts of clay in various colours (around 50g/1¾oz)
liquid polymer clay

Other materials and equipment

alcohol ink (bottle green) – powder (gold) – 1 water spray gun
1 square stamp with flower motif 5cm (2in) long – 1 square stamp with flower motif 3cm (1¼in) long
1 precision craft knife – 1 round paintbrush

Making the MOTIFS

Make the offcuts of clay pliable by kneading them together.

Take one-third of the clay and shape it, using a roller or the pasta machine, to form a sheet 4mm (¼in) thick. Print the motifs from the two stamps on to it, pressing firmly to make sure that all the details are transferred.

Cut out the motifs thus obtained using the craft knife. Bake the pieces following the manufacturer's instructions. This will give you your own negative stamps.

Take the remaining two-thirds of the clay and make a new sheet 7 × 11cm (2¾ × 4¼in) in area and 4mm (¼in) thick. Apply the negative stamps made earlier to this sheet: once for the large stamp (motif **A**); and three times for the small one (motifs **B**, **C** and **D**).

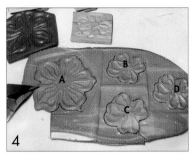

Cut out each motif using the precision craft knife.

Using the paintbrush, apply gold powder over the entire surface of the motifs, not forgetting the sides.

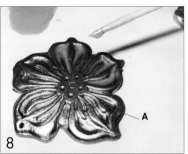

Using a needle, make a hole in motif **A** 2mm (¹⁄₁₆in) from the edge (see left). Do the same for the two small motifs **B** and **C**. Do not put a hole in the last motif, **D**, which will be for the ring.

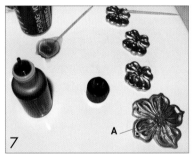

Bake the motifs according to the manufacturer's instructions. Leave each motif to cool completely, then proceed to add colour to motif **A**. Place a little liquid polymer clay and a drop of bottle green alcohol ink on to a ceramic tile. Mix the clay and the ink together carefully using a cocktail stick.

Apply the coloured clay in little dabs to the hollows of the petals of motif **A**.

Begin with the widest surface, then stretch out the clay with the cocktail stick so that it reaches even the narrowest places.

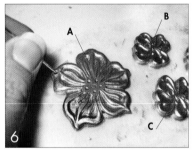

Place little drops of coloured clay on to the motif to make the stamens in the centre. Repeat the process for the small motifs **B**, **C** and **D**.

Primrose

EARRINGS
Length of earring: 5cm (2in)

2 motifs **B** and **C**
1 pair of sleepers (copper)
2 rings, diameter 5mm (copper), **Y**
2 rings, diameter 7mm (copper), **Y'**

Open a **Y'** ring using the flat-nosed pliers and thread the small motif **B** on to it.
Then slip a **Y** ring into the **Y'** ring, and close it up again using the flat-nosed pliers.
Open the small ring located at the base of one of the sleepers and slip on ring **Y**.
Close it up again in the same way.

Make the other earring as before, with motif **C**.

Make a sausage shape with the aluminium foil, then slide the shank of the ring finding on to it.

RING
Diameter: 3cm (1¼in)

1 motif **D**
1 ring finding (copper)
1 piece of aluminium foil

Apply liquid polymer clay over the bed of the ring to act as an adhesive, and gently place motif **D** on to it.

Bake the ring, and at the same time bake motifs **A**, **B** and **C** following the manufacturer's instructions.

Leave the motifs to cool, placing them on sticks (hold the ring with pliers), then apply two layers of varnish. Push the sticks into a polystyrene block as you go along. Leave to dry.

HANGING PENDANT
Length: 37cm (14½in)

1 motif **A**
1 ring, diameter 7mm (¼in) (copper), **Y'**
70cm (27½in) of black chiffon ribbon, 1.5cm (¾in) wide
70cm (27½in) of green satin ribbon, 3mm (⅛in) wide

1

Open the **Y'** ring using the flat-nosed pliers and thread it through the hole in motif **A**.

Fold the two ribbons in half together. Slide the loop thus formed into the **Y'** ring (see above).

2

Thread the ends of each ribbon back through the loop.

3

Tighten the ribbons to make a knot (see above). This technique enables you to attach a hanging pendant to a ribbon in an attractive way, hiding the ring. It also prevents the pendant from turning over.

Venice

Colour and quantity of clay used

black (60g/2oz)

Other materials and equipment

1 sachet of glass microbeads (gold)
1 sachet of glass microbeads (silver) – 1 pair of gloves

Making the BEADS

Prepare the clay by kneading it, then form it into a sausage shape 16cm (6¼in) long and 1.8cm (¾in) in diameter.

From the sausage cut the following sections:
- 6 × 1.5cm (¾in) long for beads **A**.
- 4 × 1cm (½in) long for beads **B**.
- 3 × 5mm (¼in) long for beads **C**.
Cut the rest of the sausage in half for beads **D**.

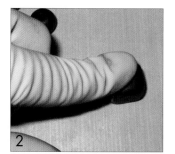
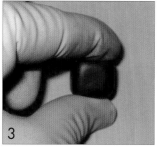

Take the sections for beads **B**. Start by making balls, then shape them into cubes by gently flattening each side with your fingers, piercing them with a needle as you go (see above).

Beads **A**, **C** and **D** are made by simply forming balls from the corresponding sections. Pierce each ball with a needle.

Place all the beads on a sheet of greaseproof paper and bake them according to the manufacturer's instructions.

Thread all the beads on to cocktail sticks to make them easier to decorate.

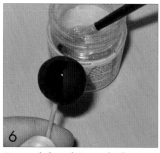

On each bead **A** apply three vertical bands of varnish, evenly spaced around the circumference of the bead, leaving three spaces without varnish (see above). Then stick on the gold microbeads, sprinkling them over each bead. Make sure that you cover all the varnish (see above).

Take the cube-shaped **B** beads and apply varnish to each face. Then decorate two faces of each bead with silver microbeads and two faces with gold microbeads.

Do not varnish the top and bottom faces of the cube.

Apply a single band of varnish to the **C** beads, going all the way around the bead from one hole to the other. Sprinkle with silver and gold microbeads. Coat half the surface of each **D** bead with varnish, then sprinkle with gold or silver microbeads.

Push each bead, mounted on a wooden stick, into a polystyrene block, as you go along. Leave to dry.

Wait until everything is completely dry before applying two layers of gloss varnish to the whole surface of each bead. By applying two layers of varnish, you will not only achieve a lacquered effect for your beads, but will also ensure that the microbeads will stay put over time.

Venice

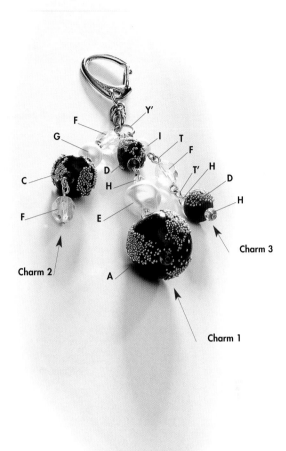

Charm 2

Charm 3

Charm 1

KEYRING

Length: 11cm (4¼in)

1 bead **A** – 1 bead **C** – 2 beads **D**
1 pearly baroque bead, diameter 1.2cm (white), **E**
3 iridescent, transparent, faceted beads, diameter 8mm (white) **F**
1 pearly bead, diameter 8mm (white), **G**
10 transparent beads, diameter 4mm (white), **H**
1 pearly bead, diameter 6mm (white), **I**
7 joining pins (silver) **T**: five × 2cm (¾in) long; two × 3cm (1¼in) long
3 flat head pins (silver) **T'**: two × 1.5cm (¾in) long; one × 3cm (1¼in) long
1 ring, diameter 7mm (silver), **Y'**
1 keyring shank

Start by preparing the different pins, threading beads on as follows:
- **pin 1**: thread on to a 3cm (1¼in) long **T** pin: one **H**; one **E**; one **H**
- **pin 2**: thread on to a 2cm (¾in) long **T** pin: one **H**; one **D**; one **H**
- **pin 3**: thread on to a 3cm (1¼in) long **T** pin: one **H**; one **C**; one **H**
- **pin 4**: thread on to a 2cm (¾in) long **T** pin: one **G**
- **pins 5** and **6**: thread on to a 2cm (¾in) long **T** pin: one **F**
- **pin 7**: thread on to a 2cm (¾in) long **T** pin: one **I**.

Cut off the excess from each pin, leaving just the 7mm (¼in) needed to make a loop at each end using the conical pliers. Then:
- **pin 8**: thread on to a 3cm (1¼in) long **T'** pin: one **H**; one **A**; one **H**
- **pin 9**: thread on to a 1.5cm (¾in) long **T'** pin: one **F**
- **pin 10**: thread on to a 1.5cm (¾in) long **T'** pin: one **H**; one **D**; one **H**.

Leave 7mm (¼in) free to make a loop.

Make the following three charms by attaching the pins together by their loops:
- **charm 1**: pin **8**; pin **1**; pin **2**
- **charm 2**: pin **9**; pin **3**; pin **4**; pin **5**
- **charm 3**: pin **10**; pin **6**; pin **7**.

Open ring **Y'** and slip on the three charms you have just made. Attach everything to the keyring shank.

EARRINGS

Length of earring: 6.5cm (2½in)

2 beads **C**
2 pearly baroque beads, diameter 1.2cm (white), **E**
2 iridescent, transparent, faceted beads, diameter 8mm (white), **F**
2 transparent beads, diameter 4mm (white), **H**
2 flat head pins, 4.5cm (1¾in) long (silver), **T'**
2 rings, diameter 5mm (silver), **Y**
1 pair of fancy clip-on earrings (silver)

On to a **T'** pin thread: one **H**; one **C**; one **E**; one **F**.

Cut off the excess pin, leaving just 7mm (¼in) to make a loop using the conical pliers.

Open a **Y** ring, slip on the loop of the pin, then attach everything to the clip via the little hole located at the bottom.
Close the ring again.

Proceed in the same way for the other earring.

NECKLACE

Length: 42cm (16½in)

5 beads **A**

4 beads **B**

6 pearly baroque beads, diameter 1.2cm (white), **E**

8 iridescent, transparent, faceted beads, diameter 8mm (white), **F**

2 pearly beads, diameter 8mm (white), **G**

26 transparent beads, diameter 4mm (white), **H**

4 locking beads (silver), **p**

1 ring, diameter 5mm (silver), **Y**

1 ring, diameter 7mm (silver), **Y'**

1 lobster claw clasp (silver)

50cm (19¾in) of cable wire, diameter 0.46mm (silver)

Thread two **p** beads and a **Y'** ring on to one end of the cable wire.

Pass the wire back through the two **p** beads and crimp it with the flat-nosed pliers.

Then thread on the beads in the following order, one of each:
H; F; H; G; H; F; *H; E; H; A; H; F; H; B*.
Repeat again from * to *.
Continue with one each of: **H; E; H; A; H; E; H; B; H; F; H; A; H; E; H; B;
H; F; H; A; H; E; H; F; H; G; H; F; H.**
End with two **p** beads and one **Y** ring attached to the lobster claw clasp.
Pass the wire back through two **p** beads and some of the threaded beads.
Tighten the wire and crimp the two **p** beads with the flat-nosed pliers.
Cut off the excess wire.

Moonlight

Colour and quantity of clay used

black (30g/1oz) – liquid polymer clay

Patterns on the textured sheets

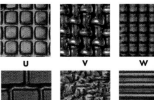

u   **v**   **w**

x   **y**   **z**

Other materials and equipment

2cm (¾in) diameter cutter – 3cm (1¼in) diameter cutter – 1 precision craft knife
1 square cutter 4cm (1½in) long – 1 round paintbrush
4 cutters, diameter 1.5cm (⅝in), in trefoil, teardrop, star and leaf shapes
metallic powder (silver, violet, midnight blue, blue and turquoise)
6 textured sheets in various patterns – 1 sheet of thin cardboard
1 ring finding – 1 hair slide finding – superglue
chiffon ribbon, 1.5cm (¾in) wide and 70cm (27½in) long, in blue and aubergine

Making the MOTIFS AND THE JEWELLERY

Hair slide: 8.5cm (3¼in) long
Hanging pendant: 20cm (7¾in) long
Earrings: 2cm (¾in) in diameter
Ring: 3cm (1¼in) in diameter

Knead the black clay to make it pliable, then roll it out to form a sheet 3mm (⅛in) thick. Apply the first textured sheet **u** to the clay and press it down firmly with a roller so that the pattern is transferred.

Use the cutters to cut out: one square **B**; one 3cm (1¼in) diameter circle **C**; and two 2cm (¾in) diameter circles **D**.

Transfer shape **A** (the hair slide) on to the sheet of thin cardboard (see pattern below) and cut around the outline using the precision craft knife. Place the template on to the clay and cut out shape **A**.

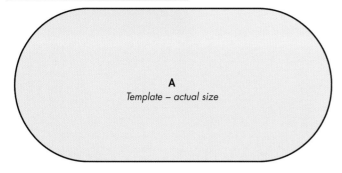

A
Template – actual size

Roll the clay out again to obtain a sheet 3mm (⅛in) thick, then apply the second textured sheet **v**.
Cut out five teardrop shapes using the relevant cutter (see left).

Repeat the same operation with the following textured sheets and cutters.

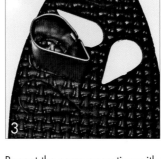

Use the third textured sheet **w** and the trefoil cutter to obtain three trefoils.

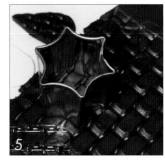

Use the fourth textured sheet **x** and the star cutter to obtain two stars.

Use the fifth textured sheet **y** and the leaf cutter to obtain two leaves.

Use the sixth textured sheet **z** and the circle cutter to obtain one circle.

Gently remove the excess clay from around the various shapes. Gather together all the offcuts of black clay and make a ball.

Place all the cut-out shapes in a cool place so that they can be handled without losing their shape.

Moonlight

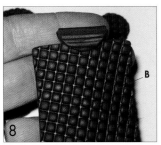

Take the grooved circle obtained by using the sixth textured sheet **z**, fold it in half, and then press it on to one side of square **B**. Pass a skewer through the two halves of the circle to create a space for the link of the hanging pendant to go through later on. Apply silver powder over the whole surface using the paintbrush.

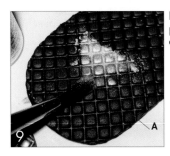

In the same way, apply silver powder to shape **A** (see left), circle **C** and the two circles **D**.

Apply the other powders in the same way to the following shapes.

Apply midnight blue powder to the teardrop shapes.

Apply violet powder to the trefoil shapes.

Apply turquoise powder to the leaf shapes.

Apply blue powder to the star shapes.

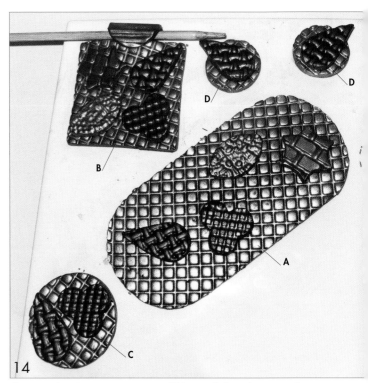

Arrange the shapes to your own liking or follow the examples given above.

Finalise the process by putting a little liquid polymer clay on the back of the pieces (stars, drops, leaves and trefoils) to be applied to shapes **A**, **B**, **C** and **D**. The liquid polymer clay acts as an adhesive.

Place shape **A** on to the finding for the hair slide, and circle **C** on to the finding for the ring (see right).

Bake all the pieces according to the manufacturer's instructions.

Attach the clip-on earrings to the **D** shapes using superglue. You could use liquid polymer clay as an adhesive instead, and then re-bake. Do the same for the other pieces.

Leave to cool, then apply two coats of varnish.

Attach the chiffon ribbons to the hanging pendant.

Rosebud

Colours and quantity of clay used

white (15g/½oz)
old rose (15g/½oz)
liquid polymer clay

Other materials and equipment

1 round 2cm (¾in) diameter cutter
1 round 3cm (1¼in) diameter cutter
1 round 4cm (1½in) diameter cutter
1 stopper or tube, diameter 1cm (½in)
1 sheet of 80g (2¾oz) paper
1 cutter in the shape of a daisy – 1 snail plate
1 pastry wheel – white adhesive – 1 flat paintbrush
1 piece of paisley-patterned paper (pink and blue)

Making the BUTTONS

Make the clay pliable by kneading it with your hands. Make a ball in each colour (white and old rose).

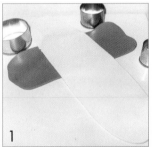

Roll out each ball using a roller or the pasta machine to obtain two sheets 2mm (¹⁄₁₆in) thick.

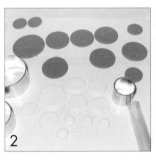

From the old rose sheet, cut out one circle using the 4cm (1½in) diameter cutter, six using the 3cm (1¼in) diameter cutter, and four using the 2cm (¾in) diameter cutter. Do the same with the white clay sheet to obtain one 3cm (1¼in) diameter circle, six 2cm (¾in) diameter circles, and four 1cm (½in) diameter circles made using the stopper or tube.

Place the various circles in a cool place so that they are easier to work with. Lay the white 3cm (1¼in) diameter circle on to the pink 4cm (1½in) diameter circle (shape **A**), the white 2cm (¾in) diameter circles on to the pink 3cm (1¼in) diameter circles (shape **B**), and the white 1cm (½in) diameter circles on to the pink 2cm (¾in) diameter circles (shape **C**). You will have one shape **A**, six **B** shapes and four **C** shapes.

Gently smooth the shapes with your finger to ensure that everything is stuck together perfectly.

Take the paisley-patterned paper and place it on to the 80g (2¾oz) paper to make it thicker for cutting. Then cut out thirteen daisies using the daisy-shaped cutter.

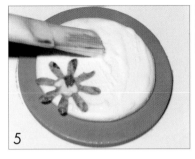

Using the paintbrush, apply some adhesive to the white part of each clay shape, and then stick the daisies on.

Use a cutting blade or a knife to help you place the daisies more easily.

Gently smooth the daisies with your finger so that they stick correctly to the white clay.

Start to decorate the old rose clay part using the pastry wheel by moving along each edge in a regular fashion.

Using a needle, make two central holes (as for buttons) in all the shapes other than the **C** shapes. Add a hole 2mm (¹⁄₁₆in) from the edge for two **B** shapes (these will be used for the earrings).

Place the shapes (apart from the **C** shapes) into the depressions of the snail plate, decorated face downwards (see above), to give them a curved shape.

Rosebud

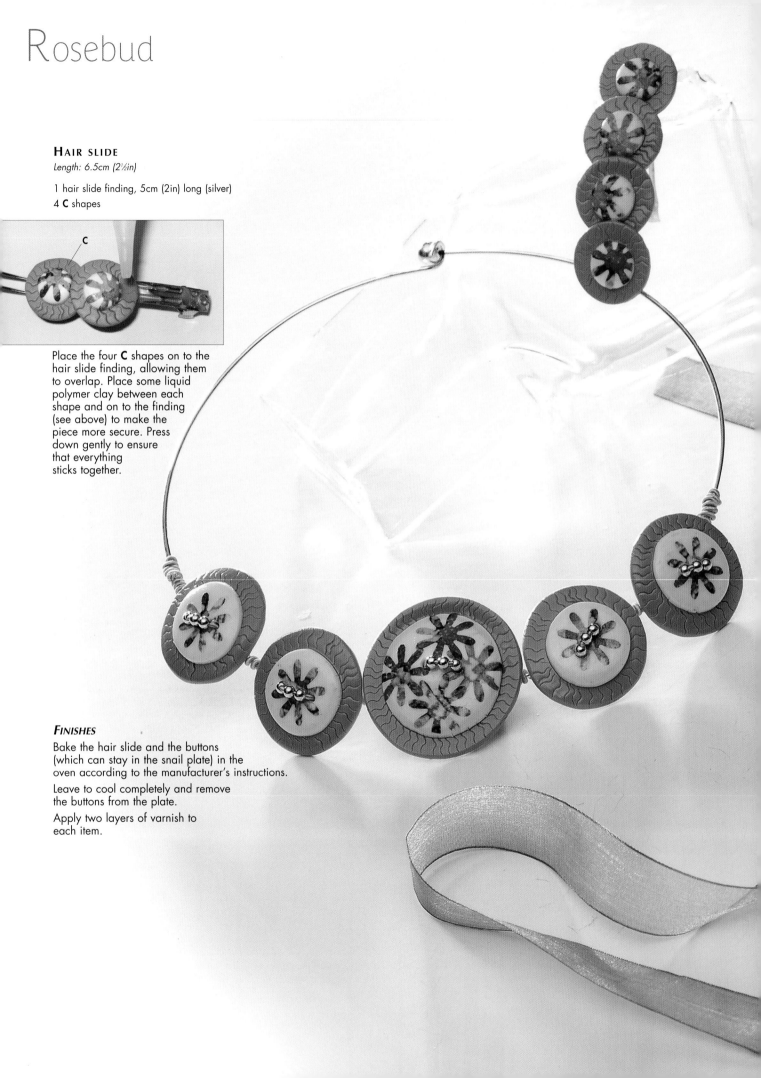

HAIR SLIDE

Length: 6.5cm (2½in)

1 hair slide finding, 5cm (2in) long (silver)
4 **C** shapes

Place the four **C** shapes on to the hair slide finding, allowing them to overlap. Place some liquid polymer clay between each shape and on to the finding (see above) to make the piece more secure. Press down gently to ensure that everything sticks together.

FINISHES

Bake the hair slide and the buttons (which can stay in the snail plate) in the oven according to the manufacturer's instructions.

Leave to cool completely and remove the buttons from the plate.

Apply two layers of varnish to each item.

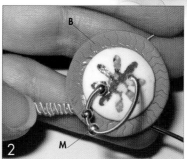

NECKLACE

Diameter: 14cm (5½in)

1 button **A** – 4 buttons **B** – 15 beads, diameter 3mm (silver), **M**
1 rigid choker necklace, diameter 14cm (5½in) (silver) – 1m (39½in) of copper wire sheathed in cotton (bonbon pink)

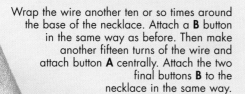

Bend the sheathed wire 2cm (¾in) from one of its ends. Place this bent part on to the choker and hold it there with your thumb. Wrap the wire three or four times around this part so that it is attached and the end is hidden (see left). Continue in this way for approximately ten turns.

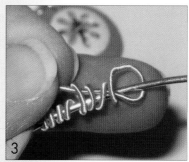

Then pass the wire through one of the holes of a button **B**, from the back. Thread on three beads **M**, and pass the wire into the second hole of button **B**, through the front. Pull gently on the wire to prevent the button from turning over.

Wrap the wire another ten or so times around the base of the necklace. Attach a **B** button in the same way as before. Then make another fifteen turns of the wire and attach button **A** centrally. Attach the two final buttons **B** to the necklace in the same way.

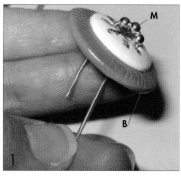

Finish with five loose turns of the wire, so that you can pass the end of the wire back through the previous turns. Then pull on this end to tighten everything up.
Cut off the excess wire. Finally, you could put some transparent nail polish on the ends.

EARRINGS

Length of earring: 4.5cm (1¾in)

2 buttons **B** – 6 beads, diameter 3mm (silver), **M** – 1 pair of sleepers (silver)
2 rings, diameter 5mm (silver), **Y** – 2 rings diameter 7mm (silver) **Y'**
16cm (6¼in) of copper wire sheathed in cotton (bonbon pink)

Open a ring **Y'** and thread on a button **B**. Close the ring again. Open a ring **Y** and slip into it the previous ring and the small ring located at the base of the sleeper. Close it up again.

Cut 8cm (3¼in) of sheathed wire, then pass the end through one of the holes of a button **B**, thread on three beads **M**, and pass the wire back through the other hole.

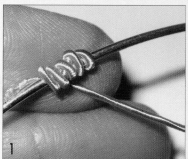

Twist the two strands of wire together at the back of the button. You can put a little bit of transparent nail polish on the ends of the wire to finish it off.
Make the other earring in the same way.

Coral

Colours and quantity of clay used

bright red (15g/½oz)
dark red (15g/½oz)
twilight orange (7.5g/¼oz)

Other materials and equipment

fine salt – flour – 1 plastic bag

Making the Beads

Make the various clays pliable by kneading them well and then making three balls.

Roll each ball on the work surface to make sausages 20cm (7¾in) in length.

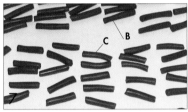

Then twist the three sausages together.

Gently roll the whole piece to obtain a new sausage 40cm (15¾in) long marbled in the three shades. Fold this in half and make another twisted sausage. Repeat this process three times to obtain very fine marbling.

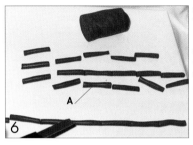

Fold the last sausage made back on itself and roll it out on the work surface, compressing each side until a length of 7cm (2¾in) is reached.

Cut this piece into three. Take one of the thirds and roll it out and stretch it to 53cm (20¾in) long with a diameter of 4–5mm (¼in). Cut it into twenty-one sections **A**, each 2.5cm (1in) long (see left).

Take another third and roll it out and stretch it to 66cm (26in) long. Cut it into thirty-three sections **B**, each 2cm (¾in) long (see left). Stretch out the final third to 70cm (27½in) long and cut it into forty-six sections **C**, each 1.5cm (⅝in) long.

In a plastic bag, mix a teaspoon of flour (to prevent the different pieces of clay from sticking to one another) and two teaspoons of fine salt (to give the clay a grainy texture).

Put all the sections in the bag, and mix well, as the salt and flour must cover every section.

Take the sections out of the bag and pinch their ends. Twist them gently so that they lose their uniform shape.

Pierce each section in the middle with a needle. Place the beads on the baking tray covered with greaseproof paper and bake them for 20–30 minutes. Leave them to cool.

Plunge the beads into water to remove the salt and flour. Leave them to dry, then apply a coat of varnish.

Coral

NECKLACE

Length: 47cm (18½in)

17 beads **A**

33 beads **B**

40 beads **C**

2 transparent, faceted beads, diameter 5mm (white), **D**

1 extender chain, 5cm (2in) long (silver)

2 locking beads (silver), **p**

1 ring, diameter 5mm (silver), **Y**

1 ring, diameter 7mm (silver), **Y'**

1 lobster claw clasp (silver)

50cm (19¾in) of cable wire, diameter 0.46mm

Thread on to one end of the cable wire one bead **p** and ring **Y**, attached to the lobster claw clasp.

Pass the wire back through bead **p** and crimp it with the flat-nosed pliers.

Then thread on one bead **D** and twenty **C** beads. Continue threading, mixing the beads **A** and **B**.

End with the other twenty **C** beads, one **D**, one **p** and the ring **Y'**, attached to the extender chain. Pass the wire back through bead **p** and crimp it with the flat-nosed pliers.

EARRINGS

Length of earring: 5cm (2in)

4 beads **A**

6 beads **C**

4 transparent, faceted beads, diameter 5mm (¼in) (white), **D**

1 pair of sleepers (silver)

1 pair of hoop (Creole) earrings (silver)

Gently open the ring of a hoop (Creole) earring, then thread on the beads in the following order: one **D**; one **C**; one **A**; one **C**; one **A**; one **C**; and one **D**.

Put the hoop earring back on its support. Close up with the flat-nosed pliers.

Open the little ring located at the base of one of the sleepers, then slip the hoop earring on to it. Close up the little ring again.

Make the other earring in the same way.

Trump heart

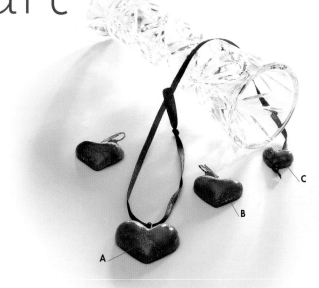

Colour and quantity of clay used

transparent white (15g/½oz)

Other materials and equipment

several sheets of gold leaf
powder (gold) – 1 round paintbrush
iridescent glitter (white)
glitter (red)
1 wax crayon (orange)
2 sticks of dry pastel (orange and red)
coloured sand (orange)
1 pliable mould with 3 hearts in different sizes
3 joining pins (gold) – 1 precision craft knife

Making the BEADS

Make the polymer clay pliable by kneading it, then roll out the clay to make a fine sheet using a roller or a pasta machine.

Then sprinkle the following elements over the sheet of clay.

Orange-coloured sand.

Iridescent white glitter.

Red glitter.

Shavings of orange wax. Grate the crayon with the blade of a knife over the clay.

Continue by adding offcuts of the sheets of gold leaf.

Press gently with your finger so that the flakes adhere well to the clay.

Sprinkle on the orange and red pastels by grating the sticks with the blade of a knife.

Finally, add the gold powder with a paintbrush.

Roll the sheet of clay up, avoiding any air bubbles.

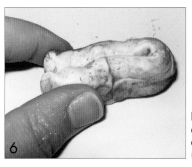

Press the sausage of clay along its length to combine everything. Fold it in half (see left).

Trump heart

Press together to obtain a sausage 5cm (2in) long.

Take the pliable mould with three different-sized hearts. Spray a little water into the mould to make it easier to remove the clay later without spoiling the shape.

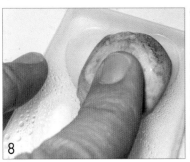

Cut the sausage in half. Take one half and place it in the large heart mould, approximately 3.5cm (1½in) in width. This will give you heart **A**.

Cut the other half into two and make two medium-sized hearts, **B** and **B'**, 2.8cm (1in) in width.

Finally, using the remaining clay, make the little heart, **C**, 1.5cm (¾in) in width.

Cut off the excess clay around each heart with the precision craft knife. Smooth the shapes with your fingers to remove any cutting marks.

Cut the pins to give you one 3cm (1¼in) long for bead **A**, and two 2cm (¾in) long for beads **B**. Pinch each pin in the middle with the conical pliers, then make into a curve by hand.

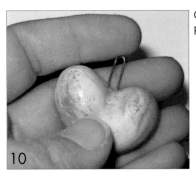

Gently insert the three curved pins into the centre of each heart.

Pierce the last heart, **C**, in the middle, lengthways, using a needle. Make the hole larger with a cocktail stick.

Bake each heart according to the manufacturer's instructions. Then plunge them into a container of iced water. The thermal shock will accentuate the transparent effect.

Wipe the beads carefully and apply two layers of varnish.

HANGING PENDANT
Length: 24cm (9½in)

1 heart **A**
1 heart **C**
1 ring, diameter 7mm (gold), **Y'**
70cm (27½in) of 3mm (⅛in) wide satin ribbon (brown)

Slip one end of the ribbon into heart **C** (see the photograph on the page opposite). You can use a needle or a piece of metal wire bent in two to help pass it through.

Then make two single knots either side of heart **C** to hold it in place.

Make a loop approximately 6cm (2¼in) in diameter at the other end of the ribbon.

Check that heart **C** will fit through the loop.

Finally, attach heart **A** to the ribbon using ring **Y'**.

EARRINGS
Length of earring: 3.5cm (1½in)

2 **B** hearts
1 pair of sleepers (gold)

Open the little loop located at the base of the sleeper and slip on heart **B** (see the photograph on the page opposite). Gently close it again using the flat-nosed pliers.

Make the other earring in the same way.

Harlequin

Colours and quantities of clay used

transparent yellow (7.5g/¼oz)

transparent orange (7.5g/¼oz)

Indian red (7.5g/¼oz)

metallic blue (7.5g/¼oz)

transparent blue (7.5g/¼oz)

mint blue (7.5g/¼oz)

navy blue (30g/1oz)

apple green (7.5g/¼oz)

raspberry pink (7.5g/¼oz)

Making the Beads

Knead the various clays on the work surface to make them pliable and then shape them into nine balls.

Roll out all the balls, except for the navy blue one, to make a sausage 6cm (2¼in) long and 6mm (¼in) in diameter.

Take three-quarters of the navy blue ball and shape it, using a roller or a pasta machine, into a sheet 6cm (2¼in) wide and 2–3mm (¹⁄₁₆–¹⁄₈in) thick.

Wrap each sausage in the navy blue sheet.

Make each sausage into a cuboid (square shape) by taking a flat object, such as a CD case, and applying it to the sausage, parallel to the work surface, exerting gentle pressure. Flatten each face of the sausage in this way, as many times as is necessary to obtain sharp corners.

Place the transparent yellow, metallic blue, apple green and raspberry pink sausages side by side, and then put the four remaining sausages (mint blue, Indian red, transparent blue and transparent orange) on top of them. Cut off the ends using the craft knife so that they are nice and straight.

Cut this rectangular block in half widthways. Lay the two sections on top of one another to make a square cane. Neaten up the ends with the craft knife where necessary.

Take the rest of the navy blue clay and make a sheet 6cm (2¼in) wide and 2–3mm (¹⁄₁₆–¹⁄₈in) thick using a roller or a pasta machine. Wrap the cane in this sheet.

Press two opposite sides of the cane with your fingers, starting at one end and exerting the same pressure until you reach the other end. Make the pressure regular to avoid misshaping the cane, although it is bound to lose its shape a little at the ends. You will now have reduced the size of the cane.

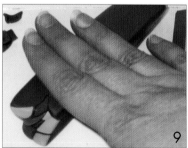

Turn the cane a quarter turn and start again on the next two sides. Continue until you have a cane with sides measuring 2cm (¾in).

Cut off the misshapen ends, retaining only the regular part of the cane. Cut ten sections 3–4mm (¹⁄₈–¼in) thick for the necklace and seven sections 5mm (¼in) thick for the bracelet and the earrings.

Harlequin

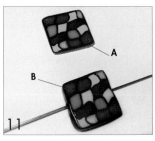

Using a needle (see left), pierce through the middle of the seven sections for the bracelet and earrings (beads **B**). Pierce the other ten sections 2mm (¹⁄₁₆in) from two opposing corners (beads **A**).

Place all the beads made on to a piece of greaseproof paper and bake them in the oven following the manufacturer's instructions.

Leave the beads to cool, then apply two layers of varnish. Use cocktail sticks to hold each bead while it is drying.

NECKLACE

Length: 42cm (16½in)

10 beads **A** – 7 iridescent beads, diameter 8mm (blue),
C 3 iridescent beads, diameter 1.2cm (blue),
D 12 rings, diameter 5mm (silver), **Y** – 22 rings, diameter 7mm (silver),
Y' 10 flat head pins (silver), **T** – 1 lobster claw clasp (silver)

Attach two rings **Y'** to each of the **A** beads. Then attach the **A** beads to each other using a ring **Y**.

Make ten charms by threading beads **C** and **D** on to the flat head pins. Make a loop at the end of each pin using the conical pliers.

Open each ring **Y** located between two beads **A** and slip on the loop of a charm. Make sure that the three charms made with a bead **D** are in the centre of the necklace, with a charm made from a bead **C** between each of them.

Attach to one end rings **Y**, **Y'** and **Y**, and then the lobster claw clasp. At the other end, attach rings **Y** and **Y'**, and then the last charm, made from a bead **C**.

BRACELET

Length: 22cm (8¾in)

5 beads **B**

6 pearly beads, diameter 8mm (blue), **C**

1 pearly bead, diameter 1.2cm (blue), **D**

3.5cm (1½in) of extender chain (silver)

2 locking beads (silver), **p**

1 ring, diameter 5mm (silver), **Y**

1 ring, diameter 7mm (silver), **Y'**

1 flat head pin (silver)

1 lobster claw clasp (silver)

25cm (9¾in) of 0.46mm diameter cable wire (silver)

Thread a locking bead **p** and the clasp on to the cable wire.

Pass the thread back through bead **p** and crimp it with the flat-nosed pliers.

Then thread on *one **C** bead, one **B** bead*. Repeat four times from * to *.

End with one **C**, one **p** and one ring **Y'** attached to the extender chain.

Pass the wire back through bead **p** and into bead **C**. Pull the wire and crimp **p** with the flat-nosed pliers.

Cut off the excess wire.

Thread bead **D** on to the pin.

Cut the end off the pin, leaving 7mm (¼in) to make a loop using the conical pliers.

Slip this charm on to ring **Y** and attach everything to the other end of the extender chain.

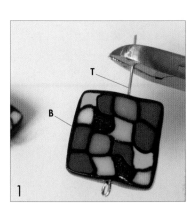

1 Make a loop at one end of a **T** pin using the conical pliers. Thread one **B** bead on to this pin. Cut off the excess at the other end of the pin, leaving just the 7mm (¼in) needed to make a loop (see above). Make the loop in the same way as before.

EARRINGS

Length of earring: 5cm (2in)

2 beads **B**

2 pearly beads, diameter 8mm (blue), **C**

2 rings, diameter 5mm (silver), **Y**

2 flat head pins (silver), **T'**

2 joining pins (silver) **T**

1 pair of sleepers (silver)

Open a ring **Y** and slip on a loop from pin **T** and the loop of a sleeper. Close the ring up again.

Thread a **C** bead on to a pin **T'**, then make a loop at the end of this pin using the conical pliers. Attach this charm to the free loop of pin **T**.

Make the other earring in the same way.

Tenderness

Colour and quantity of clay used

transparent white (150g/5¼oz)

Other materials and equipment

coloured sand (blue, pink, green and yellow)
dimensional paint (white) – 1 round paintbrush

Making the BEADS

Divide the white clay into the following quantities:
30g (1oz) to make the blue beads
45g (1½oz) to make the yellow beads
37.5g (1¼oz) to make the pink beads
37.5g (1¼oz) to make the green beads.

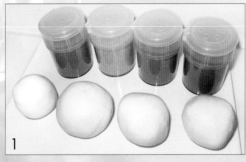

Knead each piece of polymer clay to make it pliable and shape it into balls.

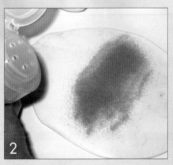

Roll out the ball of clay for making the blue beads **B** using a roller or a pasta machine. Sprinkle some blue sand on to the middle of the sheet.

Fold the sheet over and knead it so that the sand is uniformly distributed throughout the clay.

Make a sausage 14cm (5½in) long. Cut into four sections: one 6cm (2¼in) long, **B1**; one 4cm (1½in) long, **B2**; and two 2cm (¾in) long, **B3** and **B4**.

Tenderness

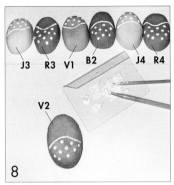

Make a ball with each sausage.

Take the ball of clay for making the yellow beads **J**, then proceed as before with the coloured sand.

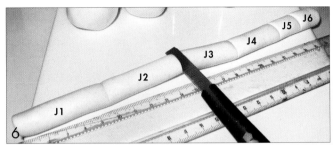

Make a sausage 22cm (8¾in) long and cut it into six sections: two 5cm (2in) long, **J1** and **J2**; two 4cm (1½in) long, **J3** and **J4**; and two 2cm (¾in) long, **J5** and **J6**. Make a ball with each section.

Take the ball of clay for making the pink beads **R** and proceed as before with the coloured sand.

Make a sausage 20cm (7¾in) long and cut it into six sections: four 4cm (1½in) long, **R1**, **R2**, **R3** and **R4**; and two 2cm (¾in) long, **R5** and **R6**. Make a ball with each section.

Take the ball of clay for making the green beads **V** and proceed as before with the coloured sand. Make a sausage 18cm (7in) long and cut it into six sections: two 4cm (1½in) long, **V1** and **V2**; two 3cm (1¼in) long, **V3** and **V4**; and two 2cm (¾in) long, **V5** and **V6**. Make a ball with each section.

Take the balls **B3**, **B4**, **J5**, **J6**, **R5**, **R6**, **V5** and **V6**. Cut each ball in half to make one **B3a** and one **B3b**, one **B4a** and one **B4b**, one **J5a** and one **J5b**, one **J6a** and one **J6b**, one **R5a** and one **R5b**, one **R6a** and one **R6b**, one **V5a** and one **V5b**, one **V6a** and one **V6b**.

Shape all the balls of clay into small oval pebbles, then assemble them as follows.
- *For the necklace*: **B1**, **J1**, **J2**, **R1**, **R2**, **V3**, **V4**, **B3a**, **B3b**, **J5a**, **J5b**, **R5a**, **R5b**, **V5a** and **V5b**, i.e. fifteen pebbles. Pierce them with a needle widthways, approximately 1cm (½in) from one end.
- *For the bracelet*: **B2**, **J3**, **J4**, **R3**, **R4**, **V1**, **V2**, i.e. seven pebbles. Pierce them twice widthways, approximately 1cm (½in) from each end.
- *For the brooch*: **B4a** and **V6a**. Pierce these with a hole lengthways. Then pierce **J6a** and **R6a** with a hole widthways.
- *For the keyring*: **B4b** and **V6b**. Pierce these with a hole lengthways. Then pierce **J6b** and **R6b** with a hole widthways.
The needle must come out of the other side of the pebble each time.

Bake the beads according to the manufacturer's instructions. Leave them to cool before moving on to the decorating stage.

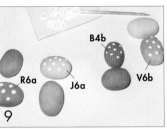

Place a blob of dimensional paint on a piece of paper and take up the amount needed with a cocktail stick (see left).

Apply a wavy line widthways around the middle of the seven beads of the bracelet (**B2**, **J3**, **J4**, **R3**, **R4**, **V1** and **V2**) and the seven central beads of the necklace (**B1**, **J1**, **J2**, **R1**, **R2**, **V3** and **V4**). Then apply some white dots either above or below each wavy line.

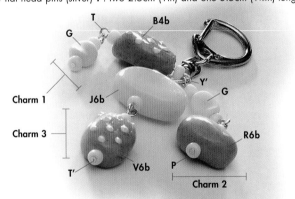

Apply little white dots to the four beads for the keyring and the brooch: **J6a**, **R6a**, **B4b** and **V6b**.

Wait until the dimensional paint is completely dry, then apply two layers of gloss varnish to all the beads, using a paintbrush.

Keyring
Length: 9cm (3½in)

1 bead (green), **V6b** – 1 bead (blue), **B4b** – 1 bead (pink), **R6b**
1 bead (yellow), **J6b** – 12 rocaille beads, diameter 3mm (white), **P**
2 crimped matt glass beads, diameter 8mm (white), **G**
1 ring, diameter 7mm (silver), **Y'** – 1 keyring shank (silver)
3 joining pins (silver) **T**: 3cm (1¼in), 3.5cm (1⅜in) and 4cm (1½in) long
3 flat head pins (silver) **T'**: two 2.5cm (1in) and one 3.5cm (1⅜in) long

Start by preparing the different pins by threading the following beads on to each of them.
- **Pin 1**: thread on to a pin **T'** 2.5cm (1in) long: one **P**; one **G**; and one **P**.
- **Pin 2**: thread on to a pin **T'** 2.5cm (1in) long: one **P**; one **R6b**; and one
- **Pin 3**: thread on to a pin **T'** 3.5cm (1⅜in) long: one **P**; one **V6b**; and one
Leave 7mm (¼in) to make a loop.
- **Pin 4**: thread on to a pin **T** 4cm (1½in) long: one **P**; one **B4b**; and one **P**
- **Pin 5**: thread on to a pin **T** 3cm (1¼in) long: one **P**; one **G**; and one **P**.
- **Pin 6**: thread on to a pin **T** 3.5cm (1⅜in) long: one **P**; one **J6b**; and one
Cut off the excess from each pin, leaving 7mm (¼in) to make a loop at each end.

Make the following three charms by arranging the pins by their loops as follo
- *Charm 1*: pin 1 and pin 4.
- *Charm 2*: pin 2 and pin 5.
- *Charm 3*: pin 3 and pin 6.

Open ring **Y'** and attach the three charms, as well as the loop of the shan of the keyring. Close up the ring again.

Tenderness

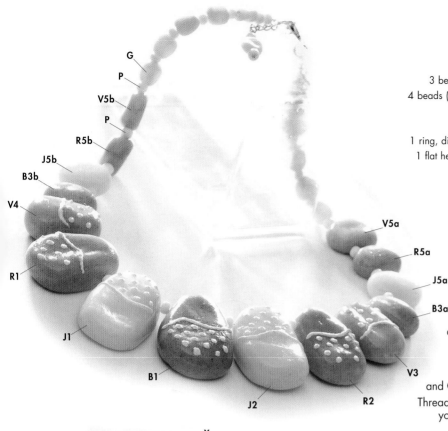

NECKLACE *Length: 47cm (18½in)*

3 beads (blue): **B1**, **B3a**, **B3b** – 4 beads (yellow): **J1**, **J2**, **J5a**, **J5b**
4 beads (pink): **R1**, **R2**, **R5a**, **R5b** – 4 beads (green): **V3**, **V4**, **V5a**, **V5b**
29 rocaille beads, diameter 3mm (white), **P**
11 crimped matt glass beads, diameter 8mm (white), **G**
1 ring, diameter 5mm (copper), **Y** – 1 ring, diameter 7mm (copper), **Y'**
1 flat head pin, **T'** – 4 locking beads, **p** – 1 lobster claw clasp (silver)
1 extender chain, 2.5cm (1in) long (silver)
50cm (19¾in) of 0.46mm diameter cable wire (silver)

Take the cable wire and thread on to one end of it two **p** beads and the ring **Y'**. Pass the thread back through the two **p** beads and then crimp these using the flat-nosed pliers. Then thread two **P**, one **G**, *one **P**, one **G***. Repeat three times from * to *, then continue with one **P** bead, the **V5b** bead, a **P**, the **R5b**, a **P**, the **J5b**, a **P**, the **B3b**, a **P**, the **V4**, a **P**, the **R1**, a **P**, the **J1**, a **P**, the **B1**, a **P**, the **J2**, a **P**, the **R2**, a **P**, the **V3**, a **P**, the **B3a**, a **P**, the **J5a**, a **P**, the **R5a**, a **P** and the **V5a**. Thread the remaining beads on to the other half of the necklace, maintaining symmetry, but ending with a single bead **P**.

Try the necklace on to check its length. Add as many **P** and **G** beads as necessary to adjust to the size of your neck.

Thread on to one end two **p** beads and a ring **Y** on to which you have attached the clasp. Pass the wire back through the two **p** beads and into the last beads threaded. Crimp the **p** beads with the flat-nosed pliers. Cut off the excess wire. Attach the extender chain to the other end, in the ring **Y'**.

Make a decorative charm by threading on to pin **T** a **P** bead, a **G** bead and a **P** bead. Cut the end off the pin leaving 7mm (¼in) to make a single loop. Slip this on to the last ring of the extender chain.

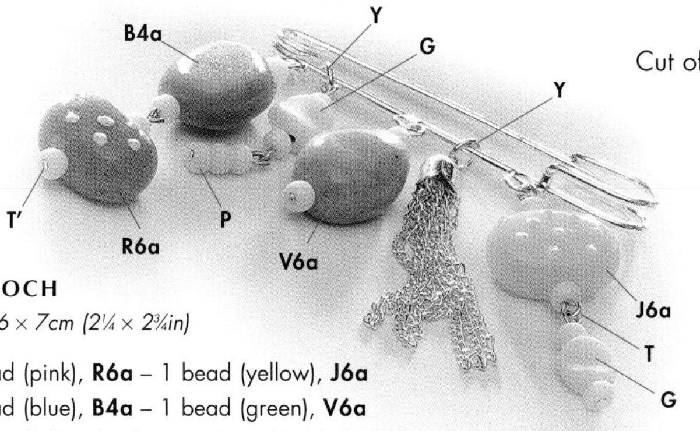

BRACELET *Length: 21cm (8¼in)*

1 bead (blue), **B2** – 2 beads (yellow), **J3** and **J4**
2 beads (pink), **R3** and **R4** – 2 beads (green), **V1** and **V2**
24 rocaille beads, diameter 3mm (⅛in) (white), **P**
1 fancy double clasp (silver)
50cm (19¾in) of 0.46mm diameter cable wire (silver)
4 locking beads (silver), **p**

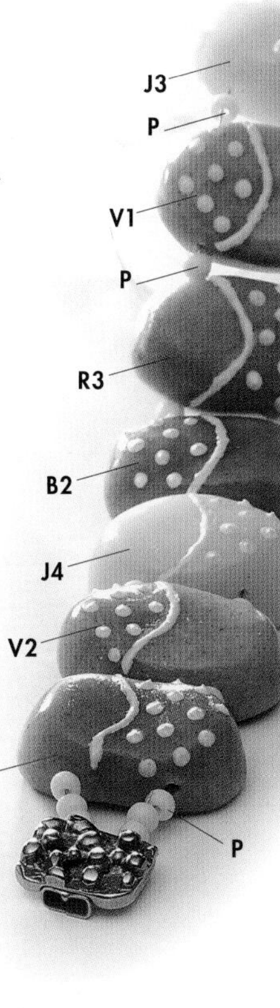

Cut the cable wire in half. Open the clasp, separating the two parts. *Thread one bead **p** on to a wire. Pass it through one of the loops of the first part of the clasp and pass 1cm (½in) of wire back through bead **p**. Crimp it using the flat-nosed pliers.

Then thread on three **P**, the **J3**, a **P**, the **V1**, a **P**, the **R3**, a **P**, the **B2**, a **P**, the **J4**, a **P**, the **V2**, a **P**, the **R4** and three **P**.

Thread on a **p** bead and pass it through the loop of the second part of the clasp. Thread the wire back through bead **p** and through some of the beads previously threaded. Tighten the wire, crimp bead **p** with the flat-nosed pliers, then cut off the excess wire*.

Repeat from * to * on the other wire to finish the bracelet.

BROOCH
Size: 6 × 7cm (2¼ × 2¾in)

1 bead (pink), **R6a** – 1 bead (yellow), **J6a**
1 bead (blue), **B4a** – 1 bead (green), **V6a**
15 rocaille beads, diameter 3mm (⅛in) (white), **P**
2 crimped matt glass beads, diameter 8mm (¼in) (white), **G**
2 rings, diameter 5mm (¼in) (copper), **Y** – 3 joining pins **T**: 3cm (1¼in) long, 3.5cm (1⅜in) long and 4cm (1½in) long
4 flat head pins **T'**: 2cm (¾in) long, 2.5cm (1in) long, 3cm (1¼in) and 3.5cm (1⅜in) long
1 chain pompom (silver) – 1 brooch 6cm (2¼in) long with 3 rings (silver)

Start by preparing the different pins, threading the following beads on to each one.
- **Pin 1**: thread on to a pin **T'** 3cm (1¼in) long: a **P**; an **R6a**; and a **P**.
- **Pin 2**: thread on to a pin **T'** 2cm (¾in) long: three **P**.
- **Pin 3**: thread on to a pin **T'** 3.5cm (1⅜in) long: a **P**; a **V6a**; and a **P**.
- **Pin 4**: thread on to a pin **T'** 2.5cm (1in) long: a **P**; a **G**; and one **P**.
Leave 7mm (¼in) to make a loop.
- **Pin 5**: thread on to a pin **T** 4cm (1½in) long: a **P**; a **B4a**; and a **P**.
- **Pin 6**: thread on to a pin **T** 3cm (1¼in) long: a **P**; a **G**; and a **P**.
- **Pin 7**: thread on to a pin **T** 3.5cm (1⅜in) long: a **P**; a **J6a**; and a **P**.

Cut off the excess for each pin, leaving 7mm (¼in) to make a loop at each end.
Make the following three charms by attaching the pins together by their loops as follows.

- **Charm 1**: **pin 1** and **pin 5**: attach this charm to the first ring of the brooch.
- **Charm 2**: **pin 2** and **pin 4**: attach this charm to a ring **Y** to be attached to the bar of the brooch.
- **Charm 3**: **pin 3**: attach this charm directly to the second ring of the brooch.
- **Charm 4**: slip the loop of the chain pompom into the second ring **Y**, then attach it to the bar of the brooch.
- **Charm 5**: **pin 6** and **pin 7**: attach this charm to the third ring of the brooch.

First published in Great Britain 2009 by Search Press Limited, Wellwood, North Farm Road, Tunbridge Wells, Kent TN2 3DR

Originally published in France 2007 by Éditions Didier Carpentier

Copyright © Éditions Didier Carpentier

English translation by Cicero Translations

English edition edited and typeset by GreenGate Publishing Services, Tonbridge, Kent

ISBN: 978-1-84448-400-3

The Publishers and author can accept no responsibility for any consequences arising from the information, advice or instructions given in this publication.

Suppliers

If you have difficulty in obtaining any of the materials and equipment mentioned in this book, then please visit the Search Press website for details of suppliers: www.searchpress.com